Finding My Groups

A Children's Story by Jed Griswold
Illustrated by Jerry Aissis

ISBN: 978-1-959957-17-1

Original story by Jed Griswold
Format, design and editing by Jed Griswold
Original watercolor illustrations by Jerry Aissis

About the Author

Dr. Jed Griswold is a published author, a retired college administrator and Professor of Psychology, a retired minister, and currently an educational and organizational consultant living in New England. For information, contact Jed at info@griswoldconsulting.net or visit www.griswoldconsulting.net

About the Illustrator

Jerry Aissis is a retired teacher who is known for bright and bold colors in his landscapes and seascapes. He teaches art classes and displays his artwork in many New England venues. "There is inspiration all around you. Never stop looking. Never stop painting." Visit https://FineArtAmerica.com

Also by this Author

A Great Retirement, Griswold Consulting
In Between, Griswold Consulting
Finding Beauty, Griswold Consulting
Finding Myself by Finding Others, Griswold Consulting
Growing Up Through Changes and Challenges, Griswold Consulting
Leafy the Leaf, Griswold Consulting
The Little Drop of Water, Griswold Consulting
The Power of Storytelling, Wood Lake Publishing
Who Haunts This House? Griswold Consulting

Finding My Groups

Story by Jed Griswold

Illustrations by Jerry Aissis

Once upon a time,
a very, very
long time ago,

every forest,
jungle, desert –
and even
every body of water -
had a special
Council of Elders.

Every year,
the local Councils
from all over
the earth
would gather
for a big meeting
to discuss ways to help
everyone work
together.

One year,
the gathered Councils
were asked
to organize
all the creatures
around the globe,
into three
separate groups ...
of the
air, land and water.

The Council set a day
for everyone to report
which group
they belonged to.

On that day,
a large number
of different
living beings gathered
from every sky,
land and water.

Each waited
for their turn
to answer
this question,

"which group
do you belong to?"

The first creature
in line
moved forward.

"Group?"
the Council asked.

"I am of the air."

"Specific type?" --

"Hummingbird"

A Council member
wrote that
in a big
"Book of Groups"

"Next..."

The next creature
in line
moved forward.

"Group?"
the Council asked.

"I am of the land"

"Specific type?"

"Elephant"

A Council member
wrote that
in the big
"Book of Groups"

"Next!"

The next creature
in line
moved forward.

"Group?"
the Council asked.

"I am of the water"

"Specific type?"

"Dolphin"

A Council member
wrote that
in the big "Book of
Groups"

"Next!"

All went smoothly,

Until...

One particular
creature
came forward.

"Group?"
the Council asked.

"Of the air"

But before
the Council
could ask
the next question,
the creature
kept talking ...

"I mean, I think
I am of the air,
because
I have wings
for flying."

"But I also have feet for walking, so I may be of the land.'

The Council
looked confused,
but the creature
kept talking ...

"And I
might also
be in the
water group,"

"Because I have special feathers on my body for swimming"

"And my feet
are shaped
to help me walk --
I mean, swim --
in the water."

The Council
was even
more confused
and they said,

"You can't be in
all three groups!
You must choose
only one."

But one of the Council members suggested a meeting to discuss it.

Listening
to each other
is often
a sign of wisdom

And after a while,
the Council returned
and announced,

"We are thankful
for this day,
because
you have taught us
a valuable lesson."

"You don't have to
belong to
just one group."

"What shall
we call you?"

"Ducky"

And that day
the Council of Elders,
and all
the creatures
of the earth,
celebrated
the wonderful
differences
within creation.

It happened
that a cloud
watched
the celebration
from high
up in the sky.

It was so happy,
it started to have
tear drops of joy,
which could
have dropped
into water,
or perhaps
onto land,
or both.

It was then
that the cloud realized

that it, too,
is a creature
of all three groups –
of the air,
the land
and the water.

And the cloud smiled
a very big smile.

What Are You Thinking About?

What is your favorite part of this story? Why?

What groups are <u>you</u> in?

What Are You Feeling?

How do you feel about the groups <u>you</u> belong to?

What will you remember about this story?

What Do You Wonder About?

Do you wonder about how Ducky felt during this experience?

Do you wonder what groups Ducky might be a part of?

Can you find all 4 creatures from the story who are hiding in the last picture of the story?

How many creatures can you find <u>here</u>?

Made in the USA
Middletown, DE
24 June 2023

33469177R00029